The Jedi Social Media Marketing Strategies:

How to Slaughter Your Competition on Platforms like YouTube, Facebook, and Instagram with little or no experience

By Stan Kennedy

©Copyright 2017 WE CANT BE BEAT LLC

Copyright 2017 by Stan Kennedy.

Published by WE CANT BE BEAT LLC

Krob817@yahoo.com

Table of Contents

Preface 5

Introduction 9

Chapter 1 Overview of the Online Ecosystem ... 23

    The Internet of Things 25

    The Framework 28

    The Economics of the Digital Platform 30

    Breakeven Profiles 32

Chapter 2 The Evolution of Communication In a Shifting Paradigm 37

    Shifting Paradigms 38

    What is Social Media? 41

    What is Twitter? 42

    What is Facebook? 43

    What is Pinterest? 46

    What is Instagram? 49

Chapter 3 How to Use Social Media 51

Chapter 4 YouTube 55

Keyword Tools 60

The Evolution of Salesmanship 62

Chapter 5 Facebook 78

Chapter 6 Instagram 95

Conclusion 102

Preface

We stand at the cusp of a fully digital society that owes its functional profile to a multitude of online platforms. From social platforms to commerce; from academic platforms to ideology, and; from financial platforms to regulatory, no stone is left unturned, no path unbeaten, in what is now an unrelenting march towards digital revolution and assimilation. So ask yourself this: Where am I in this new digital economy? Am I a player or a spectator?

We have become entirely dependent on these platforms, and rightfully so, because it is these platforms, even at this nascent stage, that has increased our efficiencies, magnified our effectiveness, accelerated our progress and thus, elevated the quality of our lives.

These online platforms are mostly related to technology, and that's true to the point that they are enabled by and depend on hardware and application technology, but what they represent is the next phase of human development and interaction. For it is these platforms that characterize our contemporary ecosystem.

Online platforms exist as a venue (the physical aspect of it), in one sense, and a method of interaction (the intellectual framework of it) in another sense. For instance, look at the various social platforms that have sprouted and evolved. While the corporate world seems to be moving toward big data, so too are educational platforms, medical platforms, entertainment platforms and all forms of commercial and social interactions that cater to large numbers of people spanning vast distances and diverse lands spread across the globe. Within the last decade alone, these platforms have gone from non-existent, to be the clarion call for a paradigm change in commerce and wealth creation.

We must remember that platforms essentially bring together two groups - a buyer in search of a seller; and a seller in search of a buyer; or a teacher in search of a student, and a student in need of a teacher. You can pair the two groups across any industry and you see the idea holds - that is the nature of the platform. The fact that it is now digital is what completely changes the landscape.

To use a more dated analogy - you can think of it as the town square or the marketplace, but with a larger, more global scope.

The platforms that exist now, are like infants in every sense of the word. We have a long way to go, and as with all things, there will be mistakes to be made, experiences to be learned, and improvements to be instituted.

We embark on an analysis of the current state of these digital platforms and review their effect on the total system. The effects, needless to say, have been all-pervasive and all-consuming. This fact alone, demands that we seek to understand and advance this subject consciously and effectively.

As we step into the future and explore new landscapes it occurs to me that the wisest of all fictional creatures I know has always imparted the best advice in all things and across all fields and I have brought his advice to bear on the way I conduct my business in this digital age.

Introduction

There are twelve saying's in the movie Star Wars that apply to the social media business and it will help you change the way you see it and will help you to change the way you benefit from it. So if you're ready to let's get down and look at the twelve sayings that I have extracted from the Star Wars saga and see how we can help you change your life and turn your business around.

The first one is when Yoda tells Anakin "train yourself to let go of everything you fear to lose now."

How does that help you in social media? Well here's a thing the lot of you who have not yet adapted to social media, or have not adopted it, the reason you're doing that is that you are holding onto an old strategy. You are holding on because you're so afraid that if you let it go you have no idea how to do the business that you want to do. You're going about it all wrong. What you need to do is you need to stand up and say that you are willing to lose by letting go all of that, and when you do that you will be able to bring in new strategies that will allow you to advance your business more than you could even imagine right now.

So when Yoda told Anakin that "fearing loss makes one greedy that's in turn making want more to turn to the dark side" that's exactly what's going to happen to you if you don't train yourself to let go of the old and take on the new you will lose because the Internet will leave you behind. If you're not already on YouTube if you're not already on Instagram if you're not already on Facebook and the range of other social media channels, you're already facing extinction. You need to change that mindset and you need to get on with life with at least these three social media tools.

The second "Fear is the path the dark side; fear leads to anger, anger leads to hate, hate leads to suffering".

Now how on earth does this apply to business? I will tell you how this applies to business. Most of the time in the old paradigm there was a lot of fear between one company and the next, between one industry and the next, between one technology and the next. All this fear was about being displaced. This company feared that the technology it had would one day be obsolete and the next company that comes along will replace it.

For example look at the fuel industry. The fuel industries such a huge and burgeoning industry that it's using, or too willing to use fossil fuels, at the cost of the planet just because they don't want to let go of it for they have so much a vested in it that they don't want to embrace clean energy technologies, and in the end everyone suffers. You cannot fear displacement. You have to evolve to embrace it. If you can embrace the displacement then you will be able to latch on to the next big. In the case of the fossil fuel industry, if they had realized that they are more about energy, and not fossil fuel energy, then the moment fossil fuels became obsolete years ago, they were switched over and they would have gone on to clean fuel energy. Pollution would have been under control. They would not be fighting tooth and nail to keep that industry that is obsolete.

You must not make that same mistake. Because once you allow fear to be present, fear is going to lead you to anger, when you're angry, you're going to do things you don't really want to do. Anger leads to hate, without a doubt. It is a time-tested path that the disillusioned travel. There's a big problem with anger leading to hate because if you are in an industry where you're angry at your competitor, you're going to land up doing things you're not supposed to be doing; something illegal perhaps that could get you in trouble, but most of all you're going to do things that are going to jeopardize the entire evolution of the industry.

There are some cases that have been reported that there was sufficient technology even to three decades ago that would have easily displaced the fossil fuel industry. But what they did was, since they were so fearful, and they were so angry and had so much hatred of these new technologies because they were afraid of being displaced, that they bought the technology and buried it. And so what happens is, in the end, everyone loses. That hate eventually leads to suffering and the entire planet is right now paying for that hatred.

The next thing that is in Star Wars that you should really think about is that you must have patience. Yoda tells Luke in the Empire Strikes Back, "Patience you must have, my young Padawan" and that is absolutely right when you start off a business under the right principles with the right footing whether or not you're making mistakes you must move forward aggressively but at the same time have patience for the results of your handwork to materialize.

When you do it this way you will not make a mistake. Patience is a very powerful advocate.

Number five. "You must unlearn what you have learned." This relates back to number one all those things that you learned about you need to really analyze why especially if you are going from an industry where you work for a living to know where you want to have your own business to make a living you need to change your mindset if you remain within the mindset of being a worker a being a staff being an employee being a subordinate that mindset will never ever be able to carry you through the responsibilities of being a business owner or an entrepreneur you need to leave what you learned about your work behind you need to let it go you need to get rid of it you need to come in with fresh ideas you need to have a new perspective you need to look at things differently.

When I first got into business after leaving the working world. I had a very different view of the business world. I had the view of business from an employee's point of view, and from an employee's point of view, you're always looking at competing priorities. You inevitably look at the business and say "hey you know if I was the boss I would do this better for my staff", or "if I was the boss I do this better for my workers", or "if I was the boss I would make sure my staff got back early, came in late and made sure they had more holidays and did less work". You cannot have the mindset of a subordinate when you are the boss so you have to unlearn what you have learned. That is crucial.

Number six. One of my personal favorites. "Do or do not there is no try."

When you're in business. When you are the owner of the company. You never say that you will "try to do" something if you are going to try, don't do it. Instead, stay home.

You get up, you do, or don't do. If you are going to try, you're better off getting a job working for someone else. Someone else who is able to do, not try. Even if you don't know what the business is about you get up and you do, you be sure in your footing, you be sure in your step forward, and you do. If you stumble, you get up and you do it again. You stumble again, you get up and you do it again. But you never just leave it a try. That is the absolute wrong mindset to be in as a business owner and when you walk into do social media, advertising social media engagement. When you go online, on the Internet, that is the best place for you to learn by mistakes, so you don't try. When you try, you're making more than a mistake you having the wrong mindset to be able to do anything. Be certain, move forward and if it doesn't work try something else but don't quit.

Number seven. "Size matters not" Yoda tells Luke, "look at me, judge me by my size, do you? and well you should not, for my ally is the force and a powerful ally".

How does that apply to this? And what force is he talking about that is relevant here? Or what size, is he referring to? Well, size really doesn't matter. You can go toe to toe with someone like Amazon, or go toe to toe with someone like General Electric. If you have a business plan and you are able to get social media on your side, and you can engage directly with your customers, size does not matter. There have been so many internet billionaires that stood up against the giants of the day, and they won. The Internet gives you the power if you are willing to act.

Jeff Bezos stood up against Wal-Mart when we first expanded Amazon. Look who's winning. Steve Jobs started off with Apple facing Microsoft on the other side. Look at the industry and the players that came up. The old guards have changed, the new has come along. Size does not matter. Do not judge a company, that comes after you, by size. Do not judge a company that has gone before you because of its size. You do what you have to do.

Number eight. "The ability to speak does not make you intelligent." This is a really funny one because this is the one where Qui Gon tells Jar Jar Binks just because he can speak does not make him smart.

In the same way, just because you know what YouTube is, and you know what Instagram is, and you know what Facebook is, doesn't mean you know how to use it. You need to get up and get going but you also need to look and observe, you need to study, you need to see how it is used and how it can be used, you need to see it as much for its potential as for its ability, you need to see how you can use it to better your business and you need to see how your business can take advantage of this. Look at it from all angles. Stop seeing them from just the social angle that the typical consumer does. Step above it and look at it from the perspective of a big business.

Because these are the tools that connect you to every single buyer you want to connect with. This is revolutionary This changes everything and this gives you the opportunity to cut out the middleman and make the money for yourself.

Number nine. "Your focus determines your reality." If you do not focus on the Internet as part of your business; if you're not focused on your business in general; if you have no focus at all, and if you're just doing it haphazardly without the mindset that you need, you're going to fail. Of that, I have no doubt. If you don't get up and do what it takes; if you don't take advantage of the social media, you will fail. I'm saying it again because that is the truth - you will fail. You need to focus on building your product, you need to focus on marketing your product and you need to engage with your customer. That's your biggest focus, if you don't do it, you're done!

Number ten. "In my experience, there is no such thing as luck" this is Obi Wan telling Han Solo that there is no such thing as luck on your road to your objective.

Before the day of the Internet, before social media came around, before YouTube was the biggest thing around, and before Instagram, before Twitter, before Facebook; you know you could possibly categorize random events as luck. I can see that; I can even buy into it as a way to categorize unintended events and consequences. But in the world where you have social media, and you have a direct line where all you need is a cellphone to take you directly into your customer's living room or into your customer's pocket - there is no more luck. What you get is what you deserve, and what you deserve is directly proportional to the effort and intelligence that you put in. Because what can get directly shows whether you know what you're doing or if you're doing anything at all. There is no more luck in this business. It is about whether or not you're doing your homework. So the more you do it the more your returns. They are directly and positively correlated to what you put in.

Number eleven. "Sometimes you must let go of our pride and do what is requested of us."

There is a lot of pride that goes on into the old school of business. You may have gone to some of the best Ivy League business schools in the forty's or fifty's. You may have learned to do business the hard way and you know what merchandising is, and you know what salesmanship is and you know what promotions are. Those are the fundamental tools of knowledge you acquired. All that goes out the door now because everything has changed. The Internet and social media marketing have completely revolutionized the way business functions and relate to the consumer and customer. It has certainly changed from the way you used to know it. And you need to let go of your pride, of all the information that you know, and you need to pick up the new mantel. But here is a little secret. Just because the industry has changed that isn't mean your experience is for naught. There is a lot in your basket of experience and you just need to change your perspective to attach your experience to the new technology.

Finally. Don't get cocky. This was what Han Solo told Luke Skywalker in one of the scenes in Episode IV.

Don't get cocky once you get an understanding of things. If you get cocky, that's going to lead you to complacency and you must realize above all else the Internet is not here in its present form. It was different yesterday, it was way different a year ago, and it will be a whole new thing tomorrow. If you get cocky, you're going to make yourself obsolete by not understanding how it's evolving. You need to stay on top of the ball every day. When you do that, you're going to reap the benefits more than you can even imagine.

Chapter 1 Overview of the Online Ecosystem

There are two main ecosystems that define our man-made universe. On the one hand is the ecosystem that encompasses all that is physical, and on the other hand, there is an ecosystem that covers all the elements of intellectual effort, or rather, all the things that are not in the physical world. We, as human beings, straddle the two ecosystems by virtue of the fact that everything that you see outside of nature flows from the human mind, through the hand of man and into our world.

Take the light bulb for instance. It was an idea, at one point - and through the effort of man, in this case, Thomas Edison, that idea stepped out of the realm of thought and stepped into the physical realm of reality. Our online ecosystem is fairly reflective of this as well. In the last industrial revolution, man's ideas went from inventions to production, to improve efficiencies in which we could develop, manufacture and supply a vast array of goods once thought impossible or once unimaginable.

That revolution and the effects that stem from it are commonplace in today's world. Any amount of analysis will show that there were significant effort and investment that went into it, and that revolution formed the backbone of the eventual economy that we raised over the course of the last few generations.

Now we stand at the cusp of the next, or current, revolution and it is one that is digital. For many, who foresaw the online revolution and the tech bubble in the last decade of the 20th century, they didn't dream of how far, how deep and how expansive what followed would be.

The platform that stands now, is just the beginning and as it is, it is already massive. You can cover everything from education for mass markets to social interaction among billions of people; you even have digital platforms at the center of uprisings, like the Arab Spring. The digital revolution has touched almost every facet of the commercial value chain.

But this is just the beginning. Because what comes next is even bigger and the impact it will have on the population at large will be much higher in order of magnitude. Of course, we are talking about the internet of things. And if you can incorporate the social media now, when the Internet of Things touches you, you will be able to take super advantage of the combination of it.

The Internet of Things

IoT, or the Internet of Things, refers to the interconnectivity of objects. These objects are not just limited to smartphones and online computers but go beyond the usual and include everything from parts that make other items, to ingredients that are used in food, to machinery, vehicles, and buildings. IoT allows the tracking of goods, the performance of goods and the location and health of any object.

We said in the beginning that there are two aspects that define our man-made universe. One is the physical aspect and the other is the intellectual aspect, and that human beings stand in the overlap of the two. That applies here as well. The intellectual aspect of the man-made universe in our current time has thus far been represented by the Internet as we know it. From static information portals, where the content moves in one direction; to blogs where the content is the craft of individuals, and is mostly unidirectional with some input from the audience in terms of comments; then there are the transactional platforms, like websites where you would bank, pay your bills, check your accounts, and so forth.

Built on top of that functional, business end of the Internet, comes the social media. If you look at the original components of the early digital platform, they were centralized - meaning, one hub to x number of users connecting to that hub. In the variation of the paradigm that followed, social media essentially formed a pattern of connections made between user and user. A sort of peer to peer relationship, unlike client-server relationships.

In the short time that social media has taken off, there is now ample evidence that humans are indeed social animals because, out of the 4 Billion Internet users in the world today, more than 2 Billion are on some form of social media. In addition to that, 1.8 billion are on Facebook, by far the most popular social media of all.

Social media is indeed one aspect of social media that was not anticipated when the first internet connections came online.

However, all these Internet applications, from banking to information dissemination, even down to social interaction was intangible. It was intangible in the sense that was being exchanged, from one terminal to the next, was not physical. Ideas, concepts, knowledge - the entire information technology was an intangible phenomenon.

The Internet of Things which comes next is not intangible and in fact, very physical. The emergence of this universe changes the game yet again and makes the Internet of Everything (Internet of Things and the Internet of Information) complete. At the center of that Internet of Everything, you will find the world of social media, which is why it is absolutely imperative that you conquer that world as it matures from its current hatchling phase.

The Framework

Together, the Internet of Everything brings added value to the existing customer, increased return to the investor and better transparency to the governing bodies. It is certainly without a doubt the greatest leap in human achievement that happens to benefit the three main pillars of our society - commerce, knowledge, and government.

What most academics will tell you is that no one can seem to agree on a common framework for what a platform is or what defines its constituents. But that's because the field is rather narrow. If you the look hard at it, the Digital Platform is anything that is defined by two or more participants who have complementary responsibilities. They are complementary because what one wants the other has and they exchange their goods/service for adequate consideration. Even if the exchange forms part of a larger chain, what is important is that the exchange for effort - past, present or future, is exchanged for consideration in the present.

It turns out that three things are true for all platforms. The first is the existence of economics within the platform. Secondly, the regulatory environment that envelops it over time. Finally, there is the social platform, and in this book, that is what we will focus on

In this book, we will focus on the third - the social aspect of the platform, and more specifically, we will drill down into three main platforms within this ecosystem - YouTube, Instagram, and Facebook.

The Economics of the Digital Platform

When Henry Ford set out to streamline production of the Model T, what he was doing was nothing short of revolutionary at that time. He, essentially, organized how a vehicle was built, streamlined its processes into a literal assembly line where a coordinated series of steps, each a member of a long chain, would begin with raw material and end with a functioning car. It was organized and the time saved, and effort expended ignited a cascade beginning with cost reductions, resulting in lower prices, making cars affordable, and thereby increasing volume and revenue.

The digital platform offers us the next step extracting more profit for the same amount of work, while, at the same time expanding market share and increasing the volume and revenue.

One of the main concerns in economic theory is the concept of marginal cost - how much more do you spend on each additional output you create. It may seem like just some arcane and esoteric metric that has no basis in the reality and nuts and bolts of everyday businesses. On the contrary. When you cast the light of marginal cost on products that are well suited to the digital platform, what you find is that these digital platforms irreversibly alter the marginal cost profile.

As production increases to higher levels, of let's say a car, the marginal cost of the vehicle begins to move toward the variable cost of the vehicles - this is because all the overhead that is employed in the manufacture of the vehicles are spread over a larger number. When production increases higher still, the marginal cost then starts to move below the unit's variable cost (the cost of the unit's material and labor) due to economies of scale. This is one of the things that Henry Ford was trying to do. If you increase your output, assuming sales numbers increase as well, then what you have is an increasing level of profitability.

The problem with traditional manufacturing businesses is that you hit a hard ceiling as far as marginal costs are concerned - after a while, they taper out and there are no more positive benefits that can be squeezed out of it.

The same is essentially true with almost all businesses, except the profile varies in the shape of the inflection point and how soon, or how late it is reached. However, in social media, the parallel is observed in terms of a learning curve. You face a learning curve on the user side as well as on the business side. The user side is almost fully adept with social media, what remains is now you, as a business.

Breakeven Profiles

On the other end of the academic analysis, is the breakeven profile. While the marginal cost profile was more of a way to look at increasing profitability, the breakeven profile is about protecting against cost overruns. There is no break even for social media. Depending on the size of your company, the additional cost is not only marginal, it is inconsequential to institute but critical if not instituted.

When you look at traditional businesses, break-even costs are heaviest when there are huge fixed costs to support a business regardless of the revenue that it may generate; or when there are large startup costs involved - like when there is significant infrastructure that needs to be built or when considerable research needs to be commissioned. In many cases, these huge costs result in barriers to entry that only sovereign governments can handle for the public good. This is why certain high-cost items like utilities and telecommunications are initially undertaken by governments, before being spun off. But even this break-even profile has changed under the auspices of the contemporary digital platform. There are no capital costs to incur and no fixed costs or depreciation to calculate. Most of the infrastructure you need in terms of hardware is pay as you use.

Breakeven profiles are fairly simple to calculate. You take the total fixed cost that you would incur in a given month, then you look at the price that you are selling your product at and subtract that from the direct cost of that product. So let's say you had a restaurant and were planning on selling pizza. It cost a dollar to make a slice, and that covers the cost of the dough, the ingredients and the electricity it takes to bake it. That is your variable cost. It is variable because it changes according to how much you make. If you make ten slices, it will cost you ten times more than making a slice. If you make none, you incur zero cost.

On the other hand, you need to pay rent for the shop. Regardless of how many slices you make or sell, that cost or the premises will always endure. That is your fixed cost or your overhead. In traditional businesses, this part of the cost is significant.

Breakeven takes the margin above the direct variable cost and applies that to the total fixed cost. So, let's say it cost you one dollar to make the slice of pizza, that's your direct variable cost, then you sold that pizza for $1.50. The fifty cents above the direct cost would go toward the paying of your overhead or fixed costs. That's called the contribution margin. So, in this case, your contribution margin is fifty cents. If your fixed cost is a thousand dollars then that fifty cents need to go towards covering that thousand dollars. From here you see it will take 200 slices of pizza to cover all your overhead. That is your breakeven. It will take you a minimum of 200 slices of pizza to have no loss and no profit. Every slice above that gives you a direct profit of 50 cents.

In the brick and mortar realm of business - there is a maximum amount of profit you can extract from your fixed cost. In the case of the pizza parlor above, you can't have an infinite number of pizzas sold at the same fixed cost.

In the digital world, that profile is very different. You are able to spread your fixed resources across a greater number of customers. In the pizza case, you are limited to people who are in the area, in the digital business your limit is the whole world - especially if your product can be delivered electronically. And one of the best businesses to do that involved the dissemination of information, knowledge, experience, and skill.

Chapter 2 The Evolution of Communication In a Shifting Paradigm

The way we communicate has changed. In fact, it has changed so much that those of you who are reading this will take the word communication differently because of how communication evolved during the course of your life. If you are like me, the first thought that comes to mind at the mention of communication is - the telephone. If you were to ask someone a little younger than me, his version of communication would be the phone as well, but he would be thinking more of the cell phone. Someone a little younger than that would mean communication to be primarily within the realm of emails and websites. But we have come much further than all that because we have crossed over into highly integrated forms of communication that range from social media to always-on chatting applications.

We are not going to look at each of the elements that make up the paradigm, and we will let others do that. For our purpose, it is sufficient to just look at it from an overall trend perspective. The point is that we have gone from a restrictive one-on-one communication, that use to be cost prohibitive - i.e. the old telephones that you had to walk to the drug store to use, and which were cost prohibitive; to the point of being able to flash out 144 words to millions of your friends in a single minute.

Shifting Paradigms

The power of communication has shifted the paradigm from being in the hands of large corporations to being in the hands of anyone who has the ability to create consumable content. This is the kind of power anyone can harvest as long as they are interested. It is the kind of power that you can harvest as well, regardless of industry or sector. Whether you are selling jams to the neighborhood, or fabrics across the world, the social media principles are the same. You could even sell jams to the world at large, and not have to necessarily increase the investment in social media. That is the power of the social media and power that you need to embrace. The only thing you must know is that the key to touching everyone is based on the knowledge we impart and the perspective that gains acceptance. After all, we all have wisdom and knowledge to impart - and now with the aid of the new communication paradigm, we can touch the audience we need with our content.

The most relevant of any business that could fit into this paradigm of communication is the dissemination of knowledge and skill. As mentioned in the earlier chapter this is the realm of massive open online courses. This is where one person or a small group of persons can create content that is designed to educate, teach and impart skill of any area or topic. Everything from photography to pathology, or from biology to biometrics can be a course and packaged into e-books, HTML sites, and downloadable writings. All of this is consumable en masse. It is the easiest way to touch someone and let our product be known.

This development has one more aspect to it and that is the way the hardware has become available as a service rather than as a purchase. The combination of two concepts endemic to the 21st century - the social economy and the sharing economy, has allowed everyday Joes like you and me to be able to utilize the services of large, or small, server farms, using only what we need, when we need it. That is why we don't incur large upfront costs and it begs the question then, since cost is a nominal factor, why you are not being more aggressive in your social media push?

The mistake many people make is that they try to do everything for free. Yes, there is room for that and you can build a lot of your presence with almost zero cost, but then you will miss out on the reach that outlets like YouTube, Instagram, and Facebook.

The evolution of the ways we communicate has impacted the frequency of our communication and the duration we spend using that communication. Both have increased and that means that more people are coming online every day, and are staying longer, consuming a host of services, from commercial, to social, to educational.

What is Social Media?

Social media is a term that describes the platform that digital interactions between people use. The most popular of these tools include Facebook, Twitter, Instagram, and Pinterest. Mind you, they are only platforms. But when you combine these platforms to the increasing prevalence of on-the-go mobile devices, what you have is a highly permeable audience that you can reach out and speak to. The central hub of any marketing effort or home business owners must be social media. Because, not only is it effective, it's mostly free.

What is Twitter?

Twitter is technically a microblogging platform. The reason it's labeled 'micro' is that you are only allowed 140 characters (that includes spaces). The point is that you need to say whatever you want to say, succinctly.

Having Twitter is like having a live feed of what's happening in the things that are important to you. It's simple if you don't already know. When you are on twitter, people who want to see what you have to say will 'follow' you. Whenever you send out a tweet (a message) it goes out to all those who have followed you. Even though you only have a seemingly limited number of characters to compose your message, in practice it actually is beneficial. Short messages to get someone's attention is a lot better than a rant. Plus, you get to send pictures - it is worth more than a thousand words.

There are more than 1 billion users on the Twitter platform. More than 65% of companies in the US use it, and it commands more than 20% of the total mobile advertising budget.

Twitter is about influence. It is about how you can penetrate mindshare in as many numbers of people in the shortest time as possible. Twitter is also mobile friendly and in this instance, most smartphones have live twitter feeds. In many, if not most cases, Twitter is like a mass text messaging capability.

The key task in getting Twitter to work for you is to build a following. Twitter is also not just a standalone - you need to be able to harvest and convert that following. So it usually ties up with your blog, your website or your Facebook page.

What is Facebook?

If you recall, the whole point of adopting social media in your home business is to expand your network and generate sales leads.

When you use Facebook, you get both of those, and you get the ability to track customer feedback in real time.

Facebook has a significant number of active monthly users, which you will see in a later chapter. From this ecosystem, you will find that 61% of those people have at least 100 people in their network. 50% of all adults have over 200 friends. Most people log on to see what's going on in their immediate and extended sphere. And when one person shares you, it goes out to all their friends.

Facebook is free to sign up and simple to set up. In fact, it's so easy to do that many people do it without thinking. Before you begin, make sure you take a look at other Facebook pages and get an idea of what you want to say on your page. What you don't say, and what you display say more about you and your business that what you do say. So keep that in mind.

With the page up and running, you need to populate the page with information on the products/services you are selling and intertwine it with other interesting tidbits that you think your readers will appreciate. The thing you should also remember is that Facebook is a social site and your information is not meant to be straight-laced and pushy.

The strength of Facebook is that it makes use of the effect of relationships -"if my friend is looking at it, I want to look at it" is the kind of thinking that subconsciously passes through everyone's' mind. That's the first half of the coin. The other half is Facebook's ability to 'Like' a post or a page. When they 'Like' it, all their friends from their network will see it. This is what you want - friends "introducing" friends at a click of a button. It is pure genius really.

When one person 'Likes' your post. That like propagates through to all his network. For illustration purposes, assume he has the average 200 friends. That one click puts your post in front of 200 people. If only 50% of those people engage and 'Like' it, effectively putting it in front of their network of an average of 200 friends. 200 + (200*100) = 20200. So with one simple post, you have penetrated 20,000 people. What determines its effectiveness is the quality of your post. That is powerful - which is why you must make yourself extremely adept at using this tool.

However, it doesn't just stop there. Facebook also has some free analytic tools where you can look at how people react to your message. It even goes one step further, you can even sell right on the Facebook page. People who buy can share their experiences and that prompts people in their network to take a look at your product.

When you strike the right chord with your message, your message will penetrate deeply.

What is Pinterest?

Pinterest gives you a platform to share visual experiences. They are not so big on text, but what they lack in words they make up for in enthusiasm. Pinterest images are shared across the membership, based on the categories that a person initially chooses. So let's say you sign up and you list categories like cars, bikes, and classic aircraft as your preference, then they will send you pictures daily that suit your taste. You are free to pin those pictures to a virtual board and go back and look at them whenever you like. You can compile your pins into categories. The more people who pin your post, the more popular it becomes.

How does Pinterest help your business? Well it gives your potential customer a compelling visual that could drive them to our site to see what else they could look at or what else you have might interest them; and, it doesn't stop there.

The beauty of giving people what they want to see is that a percentage of them are in the market for something they are looking at. If you are selling bridal gowns, and feature a tremendous number of bridal gown images, that increases the chance that someone is going to pop by your page (store) because an image you posted resonated with them. Pictures cut through gender, educational, cultural and language barriers and portray the product you are selling, or the image you are trying to portray, flawlessly.

Once you have attracted your potential customer with what he wants (emphasis on what he wants) he will come to you to fulfill his purchase needs. The one thing you cannot do is look like you are selling the product. By all means, be persistent, pushy and always be closing - just don't look like you are doing all those things. Yes, of course, everyone knows you are selling it, but you do not want to position yourself in their mind as a seller, as much as you want to position yourself as an expert in the field. The photos on Pinterest act as an invitation to visit your site and so it's good for driving traffic.

Using the bridal gown example, display the images of elegance and beauty, rather than stressing what you sell. Once your choices resonate with them and they like what they see, they will trust you with their purchase. It's called building authority. Pinterest is a great way to build that authority on a subject because you do not have to convince someone you know your stuff, you just show them.

What is Instagram?

Ok, so you get the idea with Pinterest. What about Instagram? There are a whole bunch of photos here as well. What's the difference? Is one better than the other?

Well, they are very different indeed. But you cannot distinguish one as being better than the other, they are just different. On Instagram, you mostly post photos and video clips that you took yourself on your cell phone. It has that raw and down to earth feel. The photos are almost always in the moment and on the move. In contrast to Pinterest where the images posted, are polished and clean. They both serve a different purpose.

In Instagram, there are followers. When someone follows you, every time you upload an image, they get it. It's like twitter for pictures. Your followers and whoever sees your Instagram can like you and pass it on. Again, like Twitter.

There is one limitation though, Instagram only allows photos taken on a mobile device.

Seeing as the two are different, it is usually advised that you use both, but if you have to only limit yourself to one, use Instagram.

Instagram is also highly popular with the younger crowd. The average user is under 35. They have more than 150 million active users, which means you could potentially reach a wide audience.

The one thing that keeps you popular, is that your photos must be about something that people want to see, and if that subject matter coincides with what you are selling, you have a perfect match.

Chapter 3 How to Use Social Media

We have looked at a number of tools to get you on your way in setting up a home business. Before we go on, I think it's wise that we do a quick recap of where it is we are going with all this.

We have established we want to advance your business, to increase revenue, and widen profit margins. We have also determined that we want to be able to market and sell to a wide cross-section of customers.

Unlike the past, we are no longer limited to selling within our own neighborhood. You could be sitting in Juno, Alaska, but if you know how to get around the internet, you could be selling to someone in the South Pacific.

You have the tools you need to get onto Facebook, YouTube, and Instagram, now I will share a way for you to leverage all these sites to your benefit. If you work smart enough, you won't have a single cent to pay more than the price of your Internet bill to get up and running.

Start with a Facebook account and get as many people to follow you. You do this, by following them first. Many people (not all) return the courtesy and follow you back) - Now you have a small audience. If you are able to send out pithy one-liners, or interesting images and contribute positively, people in that group will "like" your post and most likely begin to follow you as well. Now you're growing your base. Keep doing this and insert yourself into conversations that you know will not offend anyone. Build on 'likes'. Go to the analytics section and see what time most of your posts are viewed. Don't post at 10 am when you see that your posts are getting read at 7 pm. Post it at the right time and you will see an uptick in viewership.

Now do the same on Twitter. Never buy followers. Build your Twitter presence, Pinterest, and Instagram in tandem. As you build and get a feel for the crowd, start giving them solutions that run in tandem with your product.

Warning: Do not start to sell your product to these people you just 'met'.

You need to build authority and you will do that with your insightful posts, attractive Pinterest images, and lots of related Instagram.

You can even start to give away things. On your Facebook, start giving away things that are related to what the group is talking about. For instance, if the group is constantly talking about trading options online, you could find a free eBook and give it away. The proviso is, that each time someone requests the e-book, you harvest an email address.

You could also offer the book to anyone who likes your Facebook page. But the material you give away in return for likes and email addresses need not be what you are selling, but only related to the demographic. For instance, if you want to target wealthy, single men for your new dating site, maybe you could offer images of exotic cars, and e-Books about the exotic car industry. Nothing to do with dating, but it hits your target market.

Now you've built your list of leads. No matter how many leads you get, keep building. You can never get enough.

Chapter 4 YouTube

The anchor of you social media push really should evolve around YouTube because YouTube has gone from being just a curiosity and something that people hang out with and watch, to being one of the most vibrant social media platforms that the Web has ever seen right now. YouTube searches rank only second to actual Google searches. That fact alone should tell you the amount of potential that is locked up within the viewership base of YouTube. It is not just about watching movies and funny videos and music videos. It is a site that has more than two billion video views that are monetized, not in a year, not in a month, but two billion monetized video views each week. So if you can harness that power of viewership, you can hit the number of clients you can't even imagine with little or no cost. And if you're not already on that network, you're leaving a tremendous amount of money on the table, and worst off, your customers who are already on there are going to be steered towards your competitor. So not only are you not growing you're going to start contracting very soon.

So there are ten steps that you need to master to be on YouTube effectively. The first is you need to define what success is. Everyone has a different yardstick for success. Some people just want people to view their videos, which is great if you're just looking for brand name penetration. Some people want them to click on something after watching the video, which is great to get your viewership up and to get traffic to your site; or you can even use it to engage your customer at a deeper more emotional level. The choice is yours, so you need to basically decide what you want to achieve with your customer.

The second step is to go in and research keywords. Google has made this very easy and it's free. All the intelligence data that they collect is available to you as a customer if you want to go in and advertise, and if you want to go in and find out what people are searching for, and use it to your benefit. So, for instance, let's say you are into fabrics, and specifically in fabrics, you are into design and fashion. You can go in and search for fabrics and find out what their viewership is you can go in and search for fabrics and see how many people are keying that into YouTube's search parameters. With that knowledge, you can understand how many people you can hope to connect with just by using YouTube for your business.

The third element is about wanting to know your competition and if you can use the initial keyword search that you got, you can start to see what your competition is also doing because how they are represented shows up in the keyword searches.

When you get into social media marketing, the first thing that you needs to use to draw your parameter is a profile of your competition. You need to get that landscape sorted out. Your competition isn't just one company, it is an entire industry. It is everyone who can give you a run for your product or can replace your product with an alternative. Just because you sell widget A doesn't mean widget B is not a competitor.

I'll give you an example if you sell black and white paintings, your competitor isn't just the shop selling black and white paintings, it also includes the shop that is selling black and white photographs. So look for products that can replace your product, as well as products that are directly producing what you are. When you have an idea of what that is you don't necessarily need to go and search for your competitor's name in the market because people are not looking for brands on the market so much as they are looking for products. Now if you are selling item A, someone's going to turn around and search for item A. If I'm looking for socks, I'm going to type in 'socks'. So when you go in and look for keywords, you look for who are competitors that pop up for the keyword. Because now your landscape is no longer just the product, your landscape is defined by the keyword and that's how these companies also charge you. They charge you based on the keyword because the keyword disguises the entire gamut of what it means. It is a name that just doesn't seem to give the gravity it deserves. But keywords are absolutely important. Once you have that keyword, and you enter that in, you see who are all the competitors going up against you. Then you get an idea of what your competition is for that keyword, so essentially what we're doing is we're defining the landscape based on the keywords users might use for the service you provide. Mind you, it may not always be what you think. If you're selling a product we go look for the keyword that defines a product and break that keyword down like you did with the keyword tool at Google and then look at the competitors that show up for that. That's your competition.

Keyword Tools

You should invest in a keyword tool application. This is because even though Google gives you the search tools you need, it doesn't give you forensic tools that you can use to gain deep insight into your competitor's actions. The premium keyword tools that you can purchase online do that and will help you dominate the keyword faster and longer.

There are a few keyword tools that I use since they are not created equal and they give me different pieces of information. I use them on Amazon, on YouTube, Facebook and other SEO campaigns that I conduct. You can do a quick search for them and find one that fits your budget. Here are the ones I prefer and use:

1. Google Keyword Tool (this is the one we have been using in our conversation above) You should get to be very familiar with this tool.

2. 7Search. This tool gives you insight into the PPC keyword that is relevant to your product and

it gives you the possible bid price for that long tail keyword that would be successful.

3. Long Tail Pro. This is the powerhouse that you need to understand and conquer your niche with the keyword that relates to your product and your business.

4. Bulk Keyword Generator. This is a broad tool and gives you the view of the landscape. I use this tool to get an idea of the keywords that I need and then from there I know which ones to drill down into.

5. SECockpit. I've used this in the past and it is a pretty advanced tool. The only reason I don't need it anymore is that I am able to do more with a mix of other services that duplicates some of the offerings here. Try it out and see if it works with your business.

6. Seed Keywords. Finally, this is the tool you can use in your arsenal to be able to find the keywords that you need to use in your content.

Once you have an idea of what that is trying to find and similarly keywords because the beauty of the Internet is not that new can just reach everyone the beauty of the Internet is your reaching the person who will be looking for your product (based on the keyword.) Think about the keyword as the hook that you thread your bait. If you have the wrong bait, you get the wrong fish - or no fish. To get a certain fish, you need a certain bait. That keyword is your bait because that's what your potential customer has the appetite for.

The Evolution of Salesmanship

We have evolved in terms of business of being slick snake oil salesman. In the past the way to sell something or to sell anything to anyone regardless of whether they want the product. The problem with that is it eventually results in a lot of returned products. There's just a lot of mess.

What you want to do is create a product that people are looking for, and if you have created that product, and you want to sell it to the person who's looking for it. That's why keywords are important. Because a person isn't going to randomly want to purchase something he has no use for. If he's looking for a breadmaker he's going to type in 'breadmaker'. He isn't going to type in something irrelevant like 'appointment'. So if he's typing that, he's in the market for that product. That's what you want to go after. And when you do that with your competitor, you can see what keyword he is going after. And you need to be on top of his efforts so that the buyer who is looking for the product sees your product before he sees your competitor's.

The next thing you want to do is you want to be able to create a really powerful message. If you understand your keyword and you create this really powerful message around that keyword, it makes a compelling case for your customer to listen to your story. If you don't make a compelling case the on is not going to listen to your story, he is going to keep on searching till he finds your competitor who is telling him a compelling story. You have the ability to whittle down your entire competitive landscape into keywords and narratives. If you can bring a keyword and say these are the people we are looking for and you show them a story that these are the people I'm going to show this story to, then what you have is a lock and key and that local key basically opens up the wealth of market share.

In YouTube terms, your content is your presentation. You need to be able to focus on creating content. If you have a budget, get a professional content creation team to get your video. If you don't have a budget, find the best way you can appeal to your customer. There is one tip that I'm going to give you: Yes, of course, they love all the special effects and the background music and the animation- all that is great. But aside from the people who go there for the entertainment value a lot of people go to YouTube to search for things they want to know more about. They are in the market to make the purchase, but they want to go in and know more about their product. And they want it to be real, so they go in and they search for something that they're looking for to get information. You must be willing to be open with your information and educate your potential customer, you must tell your audience how to do what they need to, tell them how to take advantage of your product and live a better life with it. If you can do that, then you create brand loyalty.

In the past, with old media channels, specifically TV and radio, you were not able to do that because you were limited by thirty-second commercial spots on T.V. and those used to be really expensive. Aside from production costs, you had airtime costs that would start to eat into your margins very rapidly. But with YouTube, you have none of that. You have a one-time production cost and that's it, so you can actually switch some of your budget over to production; you can make more videos; you could hit more keywords; you could get more target audience and just channel them back to your product. So once you make a really compelling video and you've covered all the keywords, you will find that cost to be minimal.

The next item and we are now at number five, is that when you put up a video on YouTube, you need to dot all your I's and cross on the T's because that's how search engines work. Yes indeed, they have become more sophisticated over the last twenty years but search engines now are limited by what you put in. They can't guess right off the bat what you've put there, so they use some of the keywords that you have put in; they look through the web, they go to the algorithm, they learn about your product, so that they can show your page or your video to someone who searching for it. You need to understand the mentality of search engines, especially in the case of YouTube, you need to understand YouTube's search engine algorithm and philosophy, which is the same philosophy as Google's search engine philosophy.

They are in business because they are a facilitator for advertising. They are the communication link between producer and consumer. And the reason they can maintain that link is that the consumer trusts that whenever they key-in a request, they get relevant answers. If Google did not prevent irrelevant material from getting on to keywords they'll be out of business in short order. And Google is not in the business of going out of business.

Google has a very stringent policy with getting spammers and non-relevant content off their pages. If you are trying to spam them and get on the results page for a particular keyword, they will know it. The best way to rank in the search results is to provide fair amounts relevant information, valuable for your customers. One of the things that Google monitors and this is very interesting, is that they monitor what a person searches for. If you do manage to spam Google and get your video up on top for a certain keyword, they may have you there but if they start to observe that each person who clicks your video doesn't finish watching the video, or they click back and go looking for something else, you're going to lose the spots in short order. That also happens if you don't have a compelling content in place, or if you have a really good description and people click on the video, they could land on the video and they watch it but within the first two minutes your content does not capture their imagination whatsoever, or you don't give them the information that they're looking for, they will leave. And soon after that, you lose that ranking. So all that time spent making the video is going to be wasted.

Stay true to that content, make it the best content you have. Give your potential audience the best information you can give them and it will work in your favor. Also, fill up all the details of that preview with as many keywords that you can think of. Don't just wait for Google to think about the keywords, you have to tell them where you want this and what the video is about. Pick out all the possible keywords you think that someone might describe your content with. Make sure you follow strong search engine optimization practices.

Next, you need to use the 'Featured Video' section. If you are absolutely certain that your video will be a major hit, get it on the featured videos list. Get the service so that your video can be seen by as many people in the shortest amount of time. If that video manages to go viral, your organic traffic will definitely outpace your paid traffic. It's going to cost you some upfront money. That's fine. But that's based on how many clicks you get. If you pay for it and no one clicks it, you don't have to actually part with your money. It's just the same as Google search engine if you're going to use YouTube and you don't pay for that featured spot you don't get the opportunity to reach out to customers who may want to see your video. But if you pay for it, you allocate a budget for it and anyone who clicks on it will then watch a video and get to know you. As far as costs, you will only incur it when they click on it but it's worth it because if that video strikes a nerve if the video captures the imagination every person that watches that video is going to pass it on to a friend. They will share it and when they share it, it starts to go viral. So don't look at it as "Hey every click is going to cost me a dollar", if you have the confidence that your video is going to do well then every dollar you spend is not based on one click - if he passes it twenty times and they pass it twenty times each, that's 400 clicks - FOR A DOLLAR! Get it? You see how the internet magnifies your efforts, well it magnifies the returns on those efforts too.

Next. Make sure you insert your links into the various videos.

I watched a lot of YouTube videos for the purpose of gathering intelligence on competitors and customers and in my experience, as I watch these videos, I come across two categories of things that you should never do. And both sit on the opposite sides of the spectrum. The first thing you should never do is overpopulate your videos with links. It is one of the most annoying things to have to sit through a video, while you're trying to get some information out of it, and be bombarded with links that are absolutely annoying. Don't do that! On the other side of the same spectrum are those who decide that they want to give away the entire video absolutely without any links and so you get to watch this entire video without having any idea where to go next. Don't do that either. There is a fine balance between too many links and zero links because, as a consumer, if you're watching a video and you're trying to get some information, every now and then knowing where to go next to get a particular piece of information really helps. If that link is not there then you're kind of leaving that audience, or that person, or that potential customer, out in the wilderness without any idea where to go to next. That's a really good way to teach them all that you can and then give them to your competitor. So make sure you insert just enough links at the appropriate point where it is convenient to them.

Leave it to them to make the decision. Now, I've seen in the old way of doing things where they have these long sales letter formats, for websites where they don't put any links on the page, and you see miles and miles of real estate endlessly going over the point, by point, by point, of how great a certain product is. And every few scrolls, you inevitably come across a sales pitch "buy now", "buy here", "don't lose out now"; you know, all that garbage. Don't do that either when it comes to videos. Yes that works for hard-sells and maybe for some products but for most products don't do that, you're going to get into a lot of trouble when you do that. However when you use YouTube videos, put the links in the appropriate place; tell them where to find more information, and then, at the site that they go to, make the sale over there. Don't force a sale on the YouTube site. It doesn't work out.

Next, number eight. One of the best things about the Internet is that they automatically separate your market for you. Your demographics are very clear. You can clearly pick who buys your product or who is going to buy your product. You can interact with high-value users, which means when you design your product and you already know that the Internet is going to be your media channel of distribution, then what you can do is segment your product. I'll give you an example. Go to the Apple website and take a look at their product they have a couple of different categories for you. They'll break it down for you and say "OK here is the iPad" And you can choose cellular, Wi-Fi or cellular + Wi-Fi. do that is because they segmented their customer base and they know exactly who is willing to pay more. The software is no different, the iOS that they use on an iPad with cellular or the one that has a Wi-Fi and cellular the software is no different. The hardware? Maybe, just a little. But it's not the difference in price that matters. It is market segmentation. If you see it from a customer's point of view, you see variety, when you see it from the seller's point of view, you should see market segmentation. They are tapping on to higher value users or higher value customers. And with Internet marketing, you can do that too. If you have a widget that provides the basic product, you can now add widget plus, and say this product has additional features; feature more stuff in your product when you're designing it because you have the ability to segment your market for high-value users and you can do that with YouTube. You can really drill down and get the exact customer you want, and it'll work in your favor.

Number nine. This is a little confusing to some people but it shouldn't be. Yes I know that YouTube is a social media it is a social platform and you can use it to interact, but every piece of video that you upload to YouTube needs to come with its own set of social media interactions which means you must be able to allow your viewer to share it in any which way he wants. He should be able to share it on Twitter; he should be able to share it on LinkedIn, and any other social media he wishes. The more he shares, the better. Because then, if you're doing a featured item or for doing a featured video and he shares it, hopefully, the next person likes it and they share it too, and will keep going down the stack.

I've given you nine items to look at when you get onto YouTube. You're not going to get a lot of this information anywhere else. The last thing that you want right now is to make sure that your videos come into categories - we're talking about content here. First you have your anchor content - that is your product, what it does, how it does it, where it comes from, a little bit about yourself, but focus on the product, focus on its features, focus on what it's solves - and you MUST tell your audience what your product solves. You must highlight their problem. Think back, why did you design that product in the first place? What were you trying to solve? Now figure out what they're trying to solve and tell them that.

And once you do that you have the attention. Those are your anchor videos. The second layer is your sales videos. These are the ones where you can create content that goes beyond just the features on the salient issues of the product. These are the areas, where you use artistry to bring in and convince them because you know they already want to buy the product, they're looking for it. They searched for that keyword and found you, so you know that they're looking for you or your product. What you need to do now is sell them, and this is your opportunity - to sell them on the product and make them click so that they can go to your website and then be sold. So that takes care of ten of the things that you need to do on YouTube. It is a major core of your push forward so make sure you get YouTube on to your arsenal. If you don't have the time to do it find a credible source, a credible company that has a track record of using YouTube and succeeding. Whatever happens, don't go without YouTube in your campaign.

Chapter 5 Facebook

Last year when I was leading a seminar about Facebook, I reported that Facebook had over a billion users. Today, as I write this, Facebook has over two billion monthly active users. I don't even know why I bother mentioning that number because it's probably going to change very soon. But as of now, that number is two billion monthly active users. That is something you need to keep in mind. There is no under medium on earth where you could potentially touch the lives of two billion users in a setting like the one that Facebook offers. Let's go one step further.

There are more than one point one billion mobile active users. Now, let's back that up a little. First of all these people are mobile and they are using. Facebook on their mobile device that tells you something about that user; second, they are daily users. Which means Facebook pushes aside all these people that log on sporadically - once a week, or twice, perhaps. They're just talking to you about the people who log on every day and there are one point one billion of them - they're active users and this was at the end of last year. That was an increase of twenty-three percent year on year.

Another statistic that is interesting: There are one point seven billion users of Facebook in general. Now, all that just says one thing, and you can put it at the back of your head and move on because if you don't put that in proper context those numbers are just a whole bunch of zeros. So let's put them in context. When you go out and target users on Facebook, you're not going to go out and try to hit every single one of the one billion users. Why? Because your product isn't catered to one billion users. Nobody's product is. It is almost impossible to find a product unless you're selling air or water, and you're the only person selling it. Only then can you hit each and every one of those people. For normal products, you need to separate your users. Out of the one point one billion users that are on there daily.

You're going to have teenagers, you are going to have twenty-somethings, you can have Millennials, you are going to have Gen X'ers. You're even going to have the older crowd. Not all of them create a demand for the same product, and it's unlikely that you have a product that reaches all of them. So what's the point of me telling you all these huge numbers? What I'm trying to impress upon you is that there are many users to choose from. This is a numbers game and you are playing the law of averages. The more users you have the higher the probability that you can find your demographic and your niche.

There are few more things you need to know about Facebook, and not just the numbers or people who use it, but you need to understand how to separate your Facebook users. For instance, between the ages of twenty-five than thirty-four, you have almost three hundred million users- to be accurate that's about thirty percent. Of all of Facebook active nearly users between that age range. Every second there are five new profiles being created. That shows you to speed that Facebook grows. Facebook users are predominantly female - remember that when you target your messages. And the highest traffic occurs between 1 and 3 P.M. in the middle of the week. Keep that in the back of your mind because if you decide to use Facebook advertising, and you want to hit the most people, that's when you should do it. The next busiest time when users are on Facebook is on Fridays when engagement there is greater than eighty percent.

You should also know, and everyone else knows this as well, that they're only about eighty-three to one hundred million fake profiles on Facebook. Compared to a billion users, eighty-three million doesn't sound like a lot, but that's ten percent, almost. Which means one in ten profiles that you're going after is a fake but the beauty about fake profiles is this: They're not actively clicking your ads and when you actually have ads. You don't want people to fake-click your ads because that would cost you money. The average time spent on Facebook is twenty minutes. And every sixty seconds on Facebook there are more than half a million comments posted. Three hundred thousand status updated and one hundred thirty-six thousand photos uploaded. There are more than four billion pieces of content shared on a daily basis. And one in five page viewed in the United States occurs on Facebook- that means across all the Internet, US users hit Facebook one out of five times. So that's enough of trivia about Facebook. Let's take a look and see how we can use tools.

There are no less than ten ways you can leverage Facebook and the users that are on there. All this time that I spent over the last two pages that are spent telling you about Facebook is meant to motivate you to get on to that form because it offers you the most target-rich environment to sell your wares. If you miss Facebook just like if you miss Facebook, you're leaving a lot on the table. The beauty about Facebook is this - you can go on and you can create a page or free. Anyone can do it. So that's the first thing to do. But just as in everything that happens within the new paradigm of electronic media you have to be very careful what you're doing just because it's free, don't jump in without thinking. Many people do that, make a mistake, they gather a couple of users and suddenly realize the whole concept they embarked upon is flawed- nothing jives, everything is out of whack, and then they need to change it. You can't do that when you're trying to create a brand and Facebook, believe it or not, is about to carry your brand. So be very careful, have a clear idea in your mind what you're going to do with it.

We also want to talk about customization. Many of us start a Facebook page, realizing how much we can do and how many people we can touch we jump in there and we get started. We think, at the back of our minds, that Facebook is all across the Internet seem pretty much the same, so there can't be a lot of choices you can make. That's the problem, even though Facebook is pretty uniform across the plain, the content that you see is unique to you, so you need to think about what you're saying so that people will take notice of your page. This is different from having a website. This medium is an iterative process they start with you on Facebook then they look at your product, conversely, they like a product they look for you on Facebook and may share you. So the process kind of builds on each other, you meet on Facebook then you look at the product and vise-versa. It goes back and forth. So your customizations are about content. You need to create excitement in your content and one of the best ways to do that is for people to get onto your wall. That's your main page. People come over there, they see who you are, then see what you do, and they see if there is information that they would like to be continuously fed. Unlike a website, they don't need to come and visit you because the moment they 'like' you, your content feeds into their wall. Do you see the genius of it here? I will tell you the genius of that: You get to push your content into as many people who like you. Why wouldn't you want a part of that action? It is one of the best things since sliced bread. So what you have to do is to make sure you have to think about your content coming on a feed along with other content the person likes. And then you want them to take action, but you don't need them to take action every time you put out a post. The purpose of your posts is to keep your brand fresh in their minds. So not everything that you post needs to be completely about your product. You have your core product and you have your periphery or your extend product. If you're selling handkerchiefs, you don't need to tell them every development in the handkerchief industry. You can actually have something there for them to read that will benefit them in their lives.

One of the things that people use currently are inspirational quotes. It has a good effect if you do it right and the reason why people do it is that if they have a good effect then what happens is that, by association, people attribute that good effect to you and your branding. So when you keep feeding them with positive quotes, you keep feeding them with uplifting messages, when the time comes and their mind has created a positive image of you, then you give them a product related post, it is easier for their mind to absorb that. Especially if they are looking for what you're offering. Now just because they're getting your feed, it doesn't mean they are seeing your feed or your post. Facebook controls what feed someone sees. It's just like Google and Amazon's link control. The search engines, within the parameters and in the case of Facebook it's not about search engine so much, but rather deciding what goes on to the feed. They tell you that everybody's feed goes on to your wall. That's not entirely true.

How the feed is adjusted is a complex algorithm that happens at the back and only Facebook knows it. One thing I can tell you is that the more you are liked by other people who had seen your posts, the more it is going to appear to other people who have followed you, or who have liked you or who have shared with you. So just because someone has clicked on your button doesn't mean that they are automatically going to see a post, they see maybe one in five posts, or one in ten posts, especially if you have a business page. Remember, for a business page not everyone sees your post until more fans like what you post. If your post is compelling enough that they click on it to like it, the algorithm watching your post says 'OK this post has something valuable that people are starting to like' and what it does is it disseminates that post out for the people, people who have interacted with you, not the ones who haven't. They don't randomly put your post on someone else's wall. The only way they even come close to doing that is if you are liked so much, they suggest your page to others who may have a similar liking.

So remember it's about the likes, you must post compiling content. If you put garbage and no one likes you consistently for the next one year or your posts are oblivious, then even the ones that you get and the ones that Facebook sends your post to will eventually stop and they might actually unlike you or dislike you and take you off their feed.

The next one is sharing content that's already online. You become the curator- every piece of content is not something that you have to create. Social media is about sharing. If someone starts to like the information that you're bringing online; let's say you read some news from a news outlet, or you read something on someone else's website and you share it, and they like it, and will start to pay more attention to the things that you share, and the more they pay attention and click on what you share the more the Facebook algorithm will show all your posts to a wider group of people. And that's what we want. So the thing that you have to do is allow your Facebook presence to grow organically.

There are two ways to do this; first of all, if you have a storefront, put your Facebook page up front at the counter or somewhere visible, and don't just write your Facebook user name or your user account. Don't do that. Use one of the IR codes where people can just scan it on their smartphone and automatically like it. So that the next time you post something it gets on their feed. If you ask them to key-in your Facebook page. It's going to be cumbersome and you don't want to burden your customers with that. The other thing that you can do is ask them to check into your business. If you have a storefront tell them to check in if they check and you give them an extra ten percent discount. You can even tie this in with your point of sale system. If they say they've checked in and they show you they've checked in, give them a three percent discount of five percent discount- give them a freebie, or give them something to get them to check in. The moment they check, in your feed starts going into their timeline -it starts updating them and you get one more additional customer that you can keep in your database.

So build that fan base. If you have enough staff, what I would suggest that you also do is that you keep at least two people on hand to post to Facebook. Make sure one person is talking about company-wide events saying, "hey here is what we are doing"," would you like to join us", "Hey, we are doing that, this is what's going on". The other staff you put on this will focus on things that should post: things that you get from other news outlets; things that you get that's going on in the in the community; things that you get that going on in the neighboring community. But don't do these randomly. You can start off by guessing what you should post, but then monitor what your post is doing. If your post is getting lots of likes, look at why you're getting a lot of likes. You'll be able to get two pieces of information from that. First, you get to understand your customer better, second, you get to understand what you should be posting.

If you're getting good results or a good number of likes because you're posting something on flower pots, don't go and post something about fighter jets the next day. It's not going to jive, use some common sense. Figure it out, or at least observe. If it doesn't work, move to the next until you get a following. So you have two different people managing the posts, one specifically to talk about the company because that's what the whole thing is about; the other one is to find things to share. Give the customer a reason to click that like button your posts that's more important; that's very, very important and keep building the final thing that you have to remember about Facebook is you want to keep building, and building, and building your fan base - that's the key, the rest is organic. All this is just so that you build your own image. What a lot of people miss out on is the actual advertising that you get to do on Facebook. Advertising on Facebook is a brilliant way of doing things. In my opinion, it is even better than, depending on the product, doing Google PPC. If you can do Pay Per Clicks on Facebook for your product, and if you can find your niche clientele -you've struck gold.

One of the strategies that I advise my clients to do all the time is to run contests and promotions using Facebook. Almost everyone carries a smartphone now. You can pass out contests where people can answer them, or comment on them, or take part in them wherever they are. Especially if they are in your store or something along those lines. You can pass out promotions through Facebook and you can click on it. All they have to do is click on it and like it. And they get a ten percent discount on some item. But run your promotions through Facebook - pay for it don't worry about getting it for free, that because it will come back to you in likes. This is all part of the promotions and advertising budget. Don't worry about always getting on for free. Make sure you allocate a budget to advertise on Facebook. Because that will come back to you also in terms of likes and you'll be able to spread your brand name by word of mouth.

The last thing that we're going to mention about Facebook is that you should take advantage of mobile users. Remember there are more than a billion mobile users and you can take advantage of that. Don't let that go and when you advertise to the mobile users especially if you're doing paid advertisements. There are a few ways of streamlining who you want to an advertisement to hit. One of the ones that you can use is to advertise to people who have already liked you. Which you can do and it has its benefits but you can also advertise to people who are the customers have locked on to. You can wedge yourself in between a potential customer and a competitor. That's one of the greatest things that you can do on Facebook and you should take advantage of that.

Chapter 6 Instagram

If I had to rate the many different social media that are out there in terms of functionality, I would rate YouTube as the highest, and Facebook as the lowest. Now mind you I'm not saying that Facebook is bad, I'm saying that Facebook is at the bottom of the top three. I would rate YouTube on top, Facebook at the bottom, and in between for the purpose of functionality, I would look at Instagram. Now here's why. People tend to consume with their eyes, meaning you can throw as much content as you want them but if they're going to have to read your content whatever you have to write and whatever they read - there's going to be a slip between what you mean and what they understand. But when you show them pictures, when you show them video, when you illustrate something to them - it catches them at a better rate than mere words. That is the reason why I put Facebook at the bottom of the list because it is more text written content, although it can be pictures because you're allowed to attach a video and so on and I rate YouTube on top because it's primarily video.

The reason Instagram comes in between is that Instagram is purely an image sharing platform. To most people, I don't need to introduce Instagram and the benefits are instantly obvious but we are talking to a broad range of people who don't really understand social media, so Instagram is as new as can be. The way it works is that they give you a free app that resides on a smartphone. Now Instagram is designed purely for smartphone user-driven photographs and images so you don't really get them on desktops and laptops. It is designed for the mobile user to snap a picture and it goes. This platform dates back to 2010 when it gained popularity because, like I said, people consume with their eyes and pictures are worth a thousand words more. Now in April of 2012 Instagram was purchased by Facebook for a billion dollars in cash and stock. And since then the user base has shot up to five hundred million or more. Now if Facebook themselves see the benefit of Instagram and the platform that it's on then you should too because like I said, 'the image is worth a thousand words the

Just with any other social media, you must be able to create a campaign that makes sense. Just as you wouldn't jump into YouTube without thinking about it and not jump into Facebook without considering it well enough don't jump into Instagram without understanding what it is and what you can do with it. Once you do, basically you just start of opening a free account and you add a profile picture whether it's a brand or a photograph of a person. And you've got to start telling them who you are and what you are doing. And as with all other social media, you've got to get people to follow you. Now when they follow you every time you post a photograph or you post an image it gets onto their feed - to use a familiar term. That's a nice way to put it is call it a feed. And when they browse their Instagram they get to see all these photographs that everyone that they have liked is followed. They get to see all those images.

The reason you need to have Instagram as part of your social media strategy is so that you can deliberately enter into the feed of a wide range of people and thereby claim your mindshare of a certain demographic market. Even if you don't see the value of Instagram, you need to be there because your competitor is, so even from just a defensive position you need to be able to stand up and stake your claim otherwise someone else is going to. And each person who follows them but doesn't follow you is a customer that you are losing.

So here are a few tips that you can do with your Instagram. Once you take a photograph on Instagram you can subject that image to a number of filters and editing tools that Instagram themselves allow you to use, so it's free. One of the reasons you see on Instagram has really well-captured photographs is not because everybody out there it's a good photographer, it's that a lot of them have taken the time to edit the image with the tools that have been provided. So, for example, you could take a filter on a poorly framed photograph. And transport that stylistically into something more creative.

If you noticed there was a movie some time ago at the box office and it was actually a private movie filmed on just a camcorder. One of the appeals of that movie which photography that looks like it was taken by an amateur and gives it a sense of reality that people in this generation crave for. You can realize that by looking at all the reality shows out there that people are looking for some form of bare knuckles reality. But in addition to that, you have a bunch of other photo editing apps you can use and create the photograph that you want and the image that you like and could project the overall idea that you want to. A lot of people out there actually have the talent to do this and don't and you're one of the people who don't, don't worry about it. You might have it, try it, if it doesn't work. there are a bunch of Instagram professionals out there. There were professionals out there that would do it for a fee. Get them to do your campaign.

The bottom line is you need to have an Instagram strategy and when you have that Instagram strategy to be able to post and you need to be able to get people to tag you and you need to be able to get interested in the kind of photographs that you upload to Instagram. The more people you can get, the better because when they share your photographs onto the social media like Facebook then their Facebook friends can see your Instagram presence. If they like what they see you will get additional followers. So you go on to Instagram for one or two reasons either you directly go to a campaign that directly touches over five hundred million users visually or for defensive purposes so that you get to keep the market that you're going after without ceding control to your competitors.

Conclusion

Remember there are a number of other social media outlets that you can use. But compared to all of them these three give you the best cross section of demographics and the best return on effort spent and resources deployed.

But the optimal return for the effort is if you can bring them in all at the same time because that way you can use a single event to launch across platforms and that will allow you the best penetration to the amount of resources spent. The beauty of having three platforms is that you get to cross promote and by cross promotion you will be able to expand the number of unique eyeballs. There are two kinds of viewership that you get via cross promotion. The first is a new audience and the other is repeat audience. Both have its value. Unique audience expands the number of people you engage with, repeat audience reinforces a person's exposure to your brand.

If you are not comfortable with the operation of social media or if you are busy with other operational matters for your business, then you should be able to find a professional who will be able to design a comprehensive campaign for you. That is always the better alternative since there is a learning curve you must go through, and time is money, right? So you may want to consider outside help. In either case, the material in this book should give you enough background insight into the different platforms to be able to move your business to the next frontier.

But if you have the time, becoming the Jedi of social media is a lucrative way to dominate any industry. Whether you are a writer and your product is the words you craft, or you are a manufacturer and the products you create are done with machines, the one common thread between them is that you need to connect with your audience and the consumer of your products.

The entire premise of social media proficiency is so that you know how to engage existing customers and connect with new ones. Here is one way you can think about it. Thirty years ago, the way to get more customers was to engage salesmen to go out in the field and speak on your behalf. That was inefficient, expensive and problematic. It caused a lot of problems because you have ineffective salesmen, you had salesmen who promise the undeliverable, and you had salesmen randomly knocking on the door of people who may not have needed your product.

But if you now, instead, put your full force into advancing your social media presence and paid sufficient attention to its engagement rates and other metrics, what you have is the ability to step aside from salesmen and the costs associated with it and instead go directly to the customer who is in search of your product.

I am not advocating the total abolishment of the sales division. There are some products that still need a salesman to meet the customer, but not at the levels that were needed a few years back. With social media, you can take control of the message that the customer hears form you, you can streamline your engagement with them and you can get real –time feedback about what your customers are saying about you to their friends. That is a huge potential that you need to get accustomed to because it helps you along every stage of your product life-cycle. Not only can you sell more, if you listen carefully, you will even be able to design products that people want more.

May the force of Social Media be with You!

www.ingramcontent.com/pod-product-compliance
Lightning Source LLC
Chambersburg PA
CBHW070305230526
45470CB00002B/734